COVER: © iStockphoto; creature: © Sergey Kandakov/Shutterstock; dog: © lineartestpilot/Shutterstock; word bubble: © lineartestpilot/Shutterstock; notepad: © Alexy Grigorev/Shutterstock; pencil: © iofoto/Shutterstock; scribble: © Transfuchsian/Shutterstock

INTERIOR:
Throughout: Word bubble: © lineartestpilot/Shutterstock; Notebook: © Roman Sotola/Shutterstock; Numbers: © Nenilkime/Shutterstock; Abstract background: © LenLis/Shutterstock; Scribble background: © Transfuchsian/Shutterstock; Word bubbles: © Tropinina Olga/Shutterstock, © Tropinina Olga/Shutterstock, © Tropinina Olga/Shutterstock; Notebook: © eob/Shutterstock; Marbled Comp book: © Chimpinski/Shutterstock; Banner: © lineartestpilot/Shutterstock; Pencil: © iofoto/Shutterstock; Burst: © Booka/Shutterstock;

Pages 2-3: Paper: © iStockphoto; Page 4: Monkey/ speech bubble: © lineartestpilot/Shutterstock; Page 5: Bear with word bubble: © lineartestpilot/Shutterstock; Page 6: Socks: © lineartestpilot/Shutterstock, Squirrel: © lineartestpilot/Shutterstock; Page 7: Pencil: © iofoto/Shutterstock, Burst: © Booka/Shutterstock, Arrows: © lineartestpilot/Shutterstock, Egg with word bubble: © lineartestpilot/Shutterstock, Frog: © lineartestpilot/Shutterstock; Pages 10-11: Elephant: © lineartestpilot/Shutterstock, Bird (wings): © lineartestpilot/Shutterstock, Rooster: © lineartestpilot/Shutterstock, Glasses: © lineartestpilot/Shutterstock, Speech bubble: © lineartestpilot/Shutterstock, Arrow: © lineartestpilot/Shutterstock; Pages 12-13: sheep: © lineartestpilot/Shutterstock, Bug: © lineartestpilot/Shutterstock, Monkey: © lineartestpilot/Shutterstock; Pages 14-15: Snake: © lineartestpilot/Shutterstock, Fish: © lineartestpilot/Shutterstock, Starfish/speech bubble: © lineartestpilot/Shutterstock; Page 17: Bee: © lineartestpilot/Shutterstock, Bee: © lineartestpilot/Shuttertstock; Pages 18-19: Bug: © lineartestpilot/Shutterstock, Car: © Svinkin/Shutterstock; Pages 20-21: Bug's word bubble: © lineartestpilot/Shutterstock; Pages 22-23: Notepad: © lineartestpilot/Shutterstock; Pages 24-25: Dog/thought bubble: © Shutterstock; Pages 26-27: Sticky note: © Tom Grundy/Shuttertstock, Stump: © lineartestpilot/Shutterstock; Pages 30-31: Book: © lineartestpilot/Shutterstock; Pages 32-33: Bunny: © lineartestpilot/Shutterstock, Skateboard: © lineartestpilot/Shutterstock, Cartoon guy: © lineartestpilot/Shutterstock; Pages 34-35: Phone: © lineartestpilot/Shutterstock, Radio with legs: © lineartestpilot/Shutterstock; Pages 36-37: Surfer: © lineartestpilot/Shutterstock; Page 39: Vampire: © lineartestpilot/Shutterstock; Page 40: Speech bubble: © lineartestpilot/Shutterstock; Pages 42-43: Gravestone: © lineartestpilot/Shutterstock, Bear teacher: © lineartestpilot/Shutterstock; Pages 44-45: Quotation marks: © lineartestpilot/Shutterstock, Fire: © lineartestpilot/Shuttertstock; Pages 46-47: Rat: © lineartestpilot/Shutterstock, Soda: © lineartestpilot/Shutterstock; Pages 48-49: Ice cream: © lineartestpilot/Shutterstock, Banana: © lineartestpilot/Shutterstock, Cartoon doctor: © lineartestpilot/Shutterstock; Page 51: Spaghetti: © lineartestpilot/Shuttertstock; Page 53: Ghost/speech bubble: © lineartestpilot/Shutterstock; Page 55: Monster: © lineartestpilot/Shutterstock; Pages 56-57: Bat: © lineartestpilot/Shutterstock, Pants: © lineartestpilot/Shuttertstock

Fred Figglehorn and all related logos, characters and elements are trademarks of and © Fee Entertainment, LLC. All rights reserved.
Published by Scholastic Inc.
SCHOLASTIC and associated logos are trademarks and/or registered trademarks of Scholastic Inc.

ISBN 978-0-545-35603-9

12 11 10 9 8 7 6 5 4 3   13 14 15 16 17/0

Designed by Becky James
Printed in the U.S.A.   40
First printing, September 2012

Hey, home dawgs!
It's FREDDDDD!!!!

Check out my new book of FRED-TASTICALLY FUNNY JOKES! Jokes about school, monsters, food, animals, books, and more – s'all here. Plus, tons of TOP TEN LISTS, like TOP TEN REASONS WHY JUDY SHOULD DATE FRED, TOP TEN NUMBERS ON FRED'S SPEED DIAL, and TOP TEN QUESTIONS THAT KEEP FRED UP AT NIGHT.

You'll also slurp up FRED'S SASSY ANSWERS TO SILLY QUESTIONS, HOW DUMB IS KEVIN?, FRED'S TO-DO LIST, and quizzes like TEST YOUR FRED I.Q.!

Woooooo-hooooooooo!
This is for you, Judy!
Hope you think it's
HACKIN' AWESOME!!!!!

Peace out,

FRED

TOP TEN

REASONS WHY JUDY SHOULD DATE FRED

Hello, Judy.

1. He brings stray animals to school.
2. He's QUITE the ladies' man.
3. It would really annoy Kevin.
4. He got a chimpanzee to impress her.
5. Unlike Kevin, Fred would NEVER ask her to watch him do push-ups.
6. He's got a white disco suit.
7. He does the Worm like nobody's business.
8. He tried to build a tunnel to her house.
9. He risked his life to rescue her barrette.
10. If you can't beat him, date him.

WHAT TIME IS IT WHEN BERTHA, KEVIN, JUDY, AND TWO SQUIRRELS ARE CHASING AFTER FRED?

Five after one.

HOW DO YOU MAKE FRED STEW?

Take away his ice cream.

WHY DID FRED GET ARRESTED FOR GRAFFITI?

He had to draw the line somewhere.

Judy: Gee, you smell good today. What do you have on?

FRED: Clean socks.

FRED: *Where'd you get those beautiful blue eyes?*
JUDY: *They came with my face.*

WHICH LETTER OF THE ALPHABET WOULD LIKE TO GO TO THE SCHOOL DANCE WITH FRED?
I would.

WHY DID FRED TEAR A PAGE OFF HIS CALENDAR?
He wanted to take the month off.

WHY DID FRED EAT THE LAMP?
His mom told him to have a light snack.

JUDY: *I got a new football for Kevin.*
FRED: *Sounds like a good trade!*

WHAT DID FRED SAY TO HIS NEIGHBOR?
"you go, squirrel!"

FRED'S FAVORITE
DUMB QUESTIONS

What time does the ten o'clock show start?

Who's buried in Grant's Tomb?

How much does it sell for at the 99-cent store?

How long do you cook a three-minute egg?

How long is Three Mile Island?

What night is Monday Night Football?

What is a snow angel made out of?

What color is orange juice?

FRED'S ANIMAL JOKES

Rhino you are, but what am I?

HOW DID THE TREE FEEL WHEN THE BEAVER LEFT?

Gnawed so good.

WHAT DO ELEPHANTS WEAR TO WEDDINGS?

Tusk-edos.

WHAT HAPPENED TO THE FROG'S CAR?

It was toad.

WHY DIDN'T THE SKUNK BUY ANYTHING AT THE MALL?

He only had one scent, and it was bad.

WHY ARE DROWNING SHARKS ALWAYS LEFT TO DIE?

Who'd give a shark mouth-to-mouth resuscitation?

WHY DID THE BALD MAN PUT A RABBIT ON HIS HEAD?

He needed the hare.

WHY DID THE SKUNK LEAVE THE RESTAURANT?

The waiter wouldn't take his odor.

WHAT SCHOOL DO GIRAFFES ATTEND?

High school.

WHAT DO WORMS LIKE BEST ABOUT THE MOVIES?

The snake previews.

WHY DIDN'T THE ELEPHANT FLY HOME FOR THE HOLIDAYS?

The airline always loses his trunk.

FAMOUS ANIMALS
IN HISTORY

Everyone's herd of these guys.

Billy Goat Clinton

Mallard Fillmore

JAWS WASHINGTON

Ape Lincoln

No rooster is above the law and no rooster is below it ...

TEDDY ROOSTERVELT

WHAT DO YOUNG WHALES JOIN?
The Boy Spouts.

HOW DO YOU START A TURTLE RACE?
"Ready, set, slow!"

WHY DO SKUNKS MAKE GOOD LEADERS?
They can stink on their feet.

WHAT JOB DID THE LION GET?
Roar-to-roar salesman.

WHAT DO YOU GET WHEN SHEEP LEARN KARATE?
Lamb chops.

WHAT PHONE SERVICE DO HIPPOS LIKE?
Call wading.

When is a sheep like a dog?

When it has fleece.

HOW IS A DOG LIKE A CELL PHONE?

They both have collar ID.

WHY DID THE MOUSE CRAWL UNDER THE DOG?

He wanted a woof over his head.

WHAT DO YOU GET WHEN A TORTOISE BLOCKS THE SUN?

A turtle eclipse.

WHAT PART OF SCHOOL DO TIGERS LIKE BEST?

Lunge time.

WHAT DID THE BOA SAY TO THE PYTHON?

"I've got a crush on you."

WHY DID FRED RETURN THE CHIMP TO THE STORE?

They had a monkey-back guarantee.

TOP TEN

ANIMALS' READING LIST

These books won't BOA you . . .

1 A Tale of Two Kitties

2 Harriet the Fly

3 Little Mouse on the Prairie

4 The Apes of Wrath

5 Moby Duck

6 The Magic School Buzz

7 Red Badger of Courage

8 Harry Otter

9 The Great Catsby

10 The Old Man and the Seahorse

ANIMALS IN SCHOOL

Gopher it!

WHAT DO COWS LIKE ABOUT SCHOOL?

Field trips.

WHY WASN'T THE GRIZZLY ALLOWED IN SCHOOL?

He had bear feet.

WHO DID THE FISH TAKE TO THE PROM?

His gill friend.

WHY DID THE TEACHER BRING BIRDSEED TO THE MEETING?

It was a parrot-teacher conference.

HOW DID THE FARMER COUNT HIS COWS?

On a cow-culator.

WHAT DID THE HORSE GET ON HIS TEST?

Hay plus.

WHAT ANIMAL HAS THE HIGHEST INTELLIGENCE?

A giraffe.

WHAT ANIMAL CAN'T STOP TALKING DURING CLASS?

A yak.

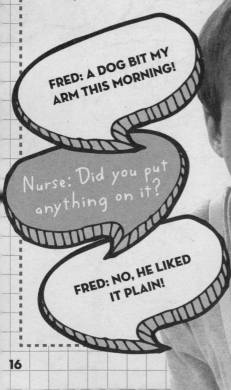

FRED: A DOG BIT MY ARM THIS MORNING!

Nurse: Did you put anything on it?

FRED: NO, HE LIKED IT PLAIN!

WHY DID THE BUTTERFLY STUDY ALGEBRA?

She wanted be a moth teacher.

WHO DO PYTHONS PLEDGE ALLEGIANCE TO?

The United Snakes of America.

HOW DID THE EARTHWORM DO IN SCHOOL?

He was at the bottom of his class.

WHY DID THE MOSQUITO JOIN A ROCK BAND?

To be the lead stinger.

KNOCK-KNOCK.

Who's there?

WORM.

Worm who?

WORM IN HERE, ISN'T IT?

KNOCK-KNOCK.

Who's there?

SNAKESKIN.

Snakeskin who?

SNAKESKIN RUN, BUT THEY CAN'T HIDE!

FRED'S FAVORITE SCHOOL JOKES

My homework ate my dog.

TEACHER: TODAY WE'RE HAVING AN I.Q. TEST.

Fred: Oh, no! I forgot to study for it.

TEACHER: WHAT'S OUR GROSS NATIONAL PRODUCT?

Fred: Broccoli?

TEACHER: WHAT DO GEORGE WASHINGTON, ABRAHAM LINCOLN, AND CHRISTOPHER COLUMBUS ALL HAVE IN COMMON?

WHY DID FRED BRING SCISSORS TO SCHOOL?

He wanted to cut class.

Fred: They were all born on a holiday.

BESIDES KEVIN, WHO ARE THE MOST POPULAR BOYS IN SCHOOL?

Art and Gym.

WHAT'S A MALL RAT'S FAVORITE SUBJECT?

Buy-ology.

TEST YOUR FRED I.Q.

No.2

1. WHO DOES FRED LOOK UP TO?

    A. MR. DEVLIN

    B. KEVIN

    C. MOM

    D. PEOPLE TALLER THAN HIM

2. WHAT'S FRED'S FAVORITE DANCE MOVE?

    A. THE HELICOPTER   **C.** THE SWIM

    B. THE WORM   **D.** THE CATERPILLAR

3. WHAT HASN'T FRED DONE TO KEVIN?

    A. BEATEN HIM OUT FOR CLASS PRESIDENT

    B. "BORROWED" HIS BIKE

    C. MET HIS SISTER

    D. TP'D HIS HOUSE

4. WHAT'S FRED'S SECRET TO MAKING A GOOD MUSIC VIDEO?

A. PRACTICE

B. HACKIN' AWESOME COSTUME

C. DRINK MUSTARD TO COAT YOUR VOCAL CORDS

D. PROFESSIONAL DANCE TRAINING

5. WHAT'S FRED'S FAVORITE SCENT?

A. VANILLA

B. LAVENDAR

C. PANCAKES

D. SWEAT SOCKS

6. WHAT SUPERPOWERS WOULD FRED LIKE TO HAVE?

A. FLY

B. TURN ANY FOOD INTO ICE CREAM

C. BECOME SQUIRREL BOY

D. ALL OF THE ABOVE

7. FRED TRIES TO KEEP A SECRET, BUT ACCIDENTALLY TELLS WHEN PEOPLE GIVE HIM . . .

A. ICE CREAM

B. MONEY

C. GARLIC SAUCE

D. A HARD TIME

8. WHAT DID FRED'S MOM FEED HIM FOR BREAKFAST?

   A. AN ANNOYING ORANGE

   B. A BOWL OF CHEERIOS

   C. A TIC-TAC

   D. A DEEP-FRIED SOCK

9. WHERE DID FRED GO ON A FIELD TRIP?

   A. A PORK-RIND FACTORY

   B. A SQUIRREL FARM

   C. A PRISON

10. WHAT'S THE ONLY THING FRED HASN'T DONE TO IMPRESS JUDY?

   A. MAKE A CAMPFIRE

   B. GET A CHIMPANZEE

   C. BUILD A FAMILY DIORAMA

   D. PUSH-UPS

Answers:
1-**D**, 2-**C**,
3-**A**, 4-**C**,
5-**C**, 6-**D**,
7-**A**, 8-**C**,
9-**A**, 10-**D**

FRED: I KNOW SOMEONE WHO IS THIRTY-FIVE AND IN FOURTH GRADE.

Kevin: Who is she?

FRED: MY TEACHER.

Why is a good math teacher like a pair of glasses?

They both improve division.

What does a school director take for a headache?

A princi-pill.

TEACHER: *We start school at 8:30 AM sharp.*
FRED: *If I'm not here, go ahead and start without me.*

TEACHER: *Sometimes I don't think you hear a word I say.*
FRED: *What?*

FRED: *Our English teacher is pretty old.*
JUDY: *Why do you say that?*
FRED: *She says she taught Shakespeare.*

WHY DID THE CLOCK GO TO THE PRINCIPAL'S OFFICE?
It tocked too much.

WHY DID FRED GET A BAD GRADE IN COOKING CLASS?

His dog ate his homework.

I didn't do it.

TOP TEN

NO-FAIL HOMEWORK EXCUSES

1. My mom baked my homework into a pie.

2. My dad used it to housebreak our puppy.

3. Too busy watching educational videos.

4. Used it for a sling when I broke my arm.

5. I belong to a religion that forbids algebra.

6. Grandma shrank it in the washing machine.

7. I threw it at someone who said you **weren't** the best teacher in school.

8. My imaginary friend borrowed my homework, and never gave it back.

9. I wrote down the assignment on my arm, and my mom made me shower.

10. It was due March 1st of **this** year?

FRED: *I'd like a new pencil.*

TEACHER: *Why?*

FRED: *This one makes too many mistakes.*

GYM TEACHER: *Tomorrow we're going to jump rope.*

FRED: *Yay! Finally I get to skip class!*

WHY DID FRED TAKE HIS REPORT TO THE SCHOOL DANCE?

The teacher told him to date his paper.

WHY DID FRED BRING A CHARGE CARD TO CLASS?

He wanted extra credit.

FRED: *I spent seven hours over my science book last night.*

JUDY: *Why? Big test today?*

FRED: *No, it fell under my bed.*

WHY DID THE TREE FLUNK ITS MATH TEST?

It was stumped.

...uh...

YOU'RE HISTORY!

S'only a test!

1. PLYMOUTH ROCK WAS . . .
   A. WHERE THE MAYFLOWER LANDED
   B. LOUD MUSIC BY PILGRIMS
   C. NOT AS CATCHY AS PLYMOUTH RAP

2. THE BOSTON TEA PARTY PROTESTED THE BRITISH . . .
   A. TEA TAX   **C.** TEA SHIRTS
   B. THUMB TAX

3. PATRICK HENRY SAID, "GIVE ME LIBERTY OR GIVE ME _____ ."
   A. SETH   **C.** DEATH
   B. BETH

4. THE BILL OF RIGHTS . . .
   A. WAS ALMOST CALLED "THE BOB OF RIGHTS"
   B. INCLUDES THE RIGHT TO BARE ARMS
   C. PROTECTS FREE SPEECH

5. THE ORIGINAL U.S. FLAG HAD THIRTEEN . . .
   A. STARS   **C.** BABY FLAGS
   B. SMILEY FACES

6. GEORGE WASHINGTON ADMITTED CHOPPING DOWN HIS FATHER'S CHERRY TREE, SAYING,
   A. "I CANNOT TELL A LIE."   **C.** "OOPS!"
   B. "MY BAD."

7. THE COLONISTS USE THE SLOGAN "NO _____ WITHOUT REPRESENTATION."

A. VACATION   **C.** PLAYSTATION
B. TAXATION

8. THE FRAMERS OF THE CONSTITUTION . . .

A. WORKED IN A FRAME SHOP
B. WENT TO THE CONSTITUTIONAL CONVENTION
C. WENT TO COMIC CON

9. WHAT DID LINCOLN AND WASHINGTON HAVE IN COMMON?

A. THEY WERE U.S. PRESIDENTS
B. THEY WERE BORN ON HOLIDAYS

10. WITHOUT THOMAS EDISON, WE WOULDN'T HAVE . . .

A. LIGHT BULBS   **C.** BOTH OF THE ABOVE
B. LIGHT BULB JOKES

11. WHAT DID PAUL REVERE SAY DURING HIS MIDNIGHT RIDE?

A. "THE BRITISH ARE COMING!"
B. "GIDDY-UP!"
C. "GIVE ME A MINUTE, MAN."

12. THE DECLARATION OF INDEPENDENCE WAS SIGNED . . .

A. IN PHILADELPHIA   **C.** AT THE BOTTOM
B. IN PHILADELPHIA CREAM CHEESE

ANSWERS: 1-A, 2-A, 3-C, 4-C, 5-A, 6-A, 7-B, 8-B, 9-A, 10-C, 11-A, 12-A

BOOKS YOU WON'T FIND IN A SCHOOL LIBRARY

HEY, EVERYBODY, SHUT UP! YOU'RE IN A LIBRARY!

Getting to School
BY MINNIE VAN

Where to Sit in Class
BY WAYNE BACK

Will He Flunk?
BY BETTY WILL

Summer Vacation
BY ANITA JOB

Dental Hygiene for Teachers
BY BRAD BREATH

How to Find Things
BY LUKE AROUND

Disgusting Cafeteria Food
BY HENRIETTA ROACH

Homework Over Spring Break
BY DEWEY HAFTA

The Old Spanish Teacher
by SEÑOR CITIZEN

The Very Long Lesson
BY DIANA BOREDOM

The Punishment
BY DEE TENSION

Learning to Bungee Jump
BY HUGO FIRST

WHY DOES THE JANITOR MOP THE FLOOR AFTER A BASKETBALL GAME?

Because the players throw up.

WHERE DO HOCKEY PLAYERS GO IN NEW YORK?

The Empire Skate Building.

KEVIN: *I can't believe I missed that goal! I could kick myself!*

FRED: *You'd probably miss.*

Fred was just about to dive off the diving board when the teacher came running up to him, shouting,

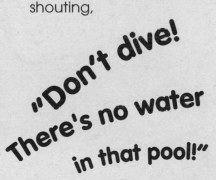

"Don't dive! There's no water in that pool!"

Fred replied,

"It's ok! I can't swim!"

TOP TEN

NUMBERS ON FRED'S SPEED DIAL

> Hello? Who is this?

1 Judy (home)

2 Judy (cell)

3 Judy (locker)

4 Bertha

5 Derf

6 Mom (work)

7 Dad (prison)

8 Ice Cream 'n' Candy 2-Go

9 Dial-a-Dance Move

10 Kevin (Not!)

FRED'S KNOCK-KNOCKS
Orange ya glad I didn't say banana?

KNOCK-KNOCK.
Who's there?
LITTLE OLD LADY.
Little old lady who?
I DIDN'T KNOW YOU KNEW HOW TO YODEL.

KNOCK-KNOCK.
Who's there?
MIST.
Mist who?
MIST YOU AT THE PARTY LAST NIGHT!

KNOCK-KNOCK.
Who's there?
BEEHIVE.
Beehive who?
BEEHIVE WHEN WE GET TO JUDY'S, OR YOU'LL BE SORRY.

KNOCK-KNOCK.

Who's there?

RADIO.

Radio who?

RADIO NOT, HERE I COME!

Knock-knock.

Who's there?
Wayne.

Wayne who?
Wayne's expected, so bwing an umbrella.

KNOCK-KNOCK.
Who's there?
HOWARD.
Howard who?
HOWARD YOU LIKE TO DO "THE WORM" WITH ME?

Knock-knock.
Who's there?
Atch.
Atch who?
Gesundheit!

Knock-knock.

Who's there?
Snow.

Snow who?
Snow use pretending you didn't hear me!

Knock-knock.
Who's there?
Oil.
Oil who?
Oil draw your picture if you pose for me.

Knock-knock.

Who's there?
Police.

Police who?
Police, no more knock-knock jokes!

KNOCK-KNOCK.

Who's there?

YA.

Ya who?

WHAT'S ALL THE CHEERING ABOUT?

X-TREME SPORTS

It's a pleasure to surf you.

WHAT HAPPENED TO THE SURFING JANITOR?

He wiped out!

WHY DON'T SKATEBOARDERS BECOME FARMERS?

They hate to bale.

WHAT KIND OF SCHOOL DO SURFERS LIKE?

Boarding school.

DID YOU HEAR ABOUT THE SKATEBOARDER ON THE MOON?

He couldn't get any air!

WHEN A SURFER GETS MARRIED, WHAT DOES HE SAY?

I dude!

WHY DID THE SURFER JOIN THE ARMY?

He wanted to surf his country.

WHAT DO YOU GET WHEN BURGLARS GO SURFING?

A crime wave.

Knock-knock.
Who's there?
Board.
Board who?
Board of surfing?
Let's go skating!

Knock-knock.
Who's there?
Seashore.
Seashore who?
Seashore tears it up out there!

TOP TEN

QUESTIONS THAT KEEP FRED UP AT NIGHT

1 How can I learn unicorn?

2 Why does Kevin always have to beat me?

3 Can money buy happiness? Or just a lot of ice cream and a big swimming pool?

4 Why are squirrels so dumb?

5 Do I have mental tilapia?

6 How can you tell if your teacher is a vampire?

7 Why would they put a vampire on a children's cereal box?

8 How long does it take Mom to remove her unibrow?

9 How can I win Judy's love?

10 Why does Mr. Devlin say "hello-ski"?

AHHHHHHH! Havin' an art attack!

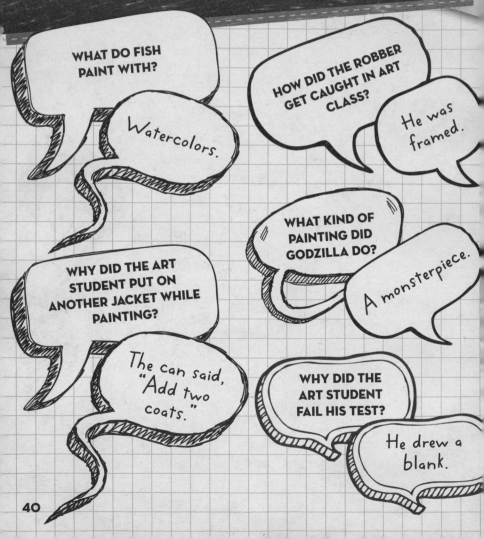

WHAT DO FISH PAINT WITH?

Watercolors.

HOW DID THE ROBBER GET CAUGHT IN ART CLASS?

He was framed.

WHAT KIND OF PAINTING DID GODZILLA DO?

A monsterpiece.

WHY DID THE ART STUDENT PUT ON ANOTHER JACKET WHILE PAINTING?

The can said, "Add two coats."

WHY DID THE ART STUDENT FAIL HIS TEST?

He drew a blank.

HOW DUMB IS KEVIN?

→ He took a ruler to bed to see how long he slept.

→ He asked the barber to make his hair longer in the back.

→ He took a baseball glove to the beach so he could catch a wave.

→ He tripped over a cordless phone.

→ He had his gold medal bronzed.

→ He threw a ball on the ground and missed.

→ He climbed over a glass wall to see what was on the other side.

→ He buried his radio because the battery was dead.

→ He went to a drive-in to see "Closed for Winter."

WORD UP

Yo! Bad spellers untie!

TEACHER: GIVE ME THE DEFINITION OF PROCRASTINATION.

Fred: I'll do it later.

DID YOU HEAR ABOUT THE KID WITH GOOD PENMANSHIP?

He got straight As.

WHY DID THE WRITER VISIT THE CEMETERY?

TEACHER: DEFINE "INTENSE."

Fred: Where Boy Scouts sleep.

R.I.P.

He needed a good plot.

TEACHER: *Give us your book report on the phone book.*
FRED: *Not much of a plot, but, boy, what a cast!*

HOW IS AN ENGLISH TEACHER LIKE A JUDGE?
They both hand out sentences.

TEACHER: *What's the difference between a bicycle and a monkey?*
FRED: *They both have wheels, except for the monkey.*

HOW DOES A BOOK ABOUT ZOMBIES BEGIN?
With a dead-ication.

JUDY: *Do you believe in animal rights?*
FRED: *No, I've never seen an animal write.*

TEACHER: *Your spelling is much better. Only three mistakes so far.*
FRED: *Thanks!*
TEACHER: *Now on to the next word.*

FRED JUST WON'T SHUT UP

Quotable quotes from Yours Truly.

"Pay no attention to those police cars."

"They must have changed all the trails since Park Ranger School."

"Never trust a zookeeper with a lazy eye."

"Maybe this fresh $1 bill will jog your memory?"

"Girls like me, Bertha. I'm hot."

"There's a lot more me where that came from."

"I didn't know how much the bus cost, so I took $25."

"Wanna play Twister?"

"Worser? That's not even a word!"

"She needs an attitude check!"

"That's when everything went black."

DID YOU HEAR ABOUT THE PIZZA THAT MADE A MOVIE?

It was panned.

WHAT DID ONE POTATO CHIP SAY TO THE OTHER?

Let's go for a dip.

BEAVER #1: *What did you eat for dinner?*
BEAVER #2: *A tree-course meal.*

HOW DOES A SODA CAN GET ENGAGED?

He pops the question.

TOP TEN

REASONS FRED LOVES ICE CREAM

I love you, too.

1. It's yummy.
2. It's delicious.
3. No time to brush? Just eat some mint chocolate chip.
4. Two words: sundae school.
5. He's always looking for a good scoop.
6. It melts in your mouth – and everywhere else
7. Tastes great with pickles and peanut butter.
8. It's sweet, like Judy.
9. In a fight, it always gets licked.
10. It's hackin' awesome!

WHAT DID ONE STRAWBERRY SAY TO ANOTHER?

How did we get into this jam?

WHY DID THE WOMAN DIVORCE THE GRAPE?

She was tired of raisin' kids.

FRED: *Will my pizza be long?*
CHEF: *No, it'll be round.*

WHY DIDN'T THE SALAD JOKE MAKE IT INTO THIS BOOK?

It got tossed.

WHY DID THE BANANA GO TO THE DOCTOR?

It wasn't peeling well.

How are we today?

WHAT DID THE APPLE TREE SAY TO THE FARMER?
Go pick on someone else.

WHAT HAPPENS WHEN YOU TELL AN EGG A JOKE?
It cracks up!

WHAT DID THE POLICE DO WITH THE HAMBURGER?
They grilled him.

KNOCK-KNOCK.
Who's there?
HAM. BACON.
Ham Bacon who?
**HAM BACON YOU
TO LET ME IN!**

KNOCK-KNOCK.
Who's there?
LETTUCE.
Lettuce who?
LETTUCE IN, WHY DON'T YOU?

KNOCK-KNOCK.
Who's there?
BUTTER.
Butter who?
BUTTER NOT TELL ANY TERRIBLE KNOCK-KNOCK JOKES!

Kevin: I feel like spaghetti.

FRED: Funny, you don't look like spaghetti.

FRED'S
TO-DO LIST

- ☐ Buy more ape chow.

- ☐ Wax Mom's back.

- ☐ Make Fredsident's Day a national holiday.

- ☐ Do The Worm.

- ☐ Buy Invisibility Cloak in every color.

- ☐ Order "Chicken with garlic sauce. Hold the chicken."

- ☐ Steal Judy's lip gloss.

- ☐ Catch Evil Fred; expose to the rest of world.

- ☐ Buy ice cream.

- ☐ Buy more ice cream.

FRED'S SCARY JOKES

Leave a message at the sound of the creep.

WHAT PART OF SCHOOL DOES THE BLOB LIKE BEST?

Show 'n' smell.

WHAT DO MUMMIES LIKE ABOUT FOOTBALL?

The post-game wrap-up.

HOW DOES A GHOST LIKE HIS HAMBURGER?

Medium scared.

WHY COULDN'T THE CANNIBAL SELL HIS HOUSE?

He was charging an arm and a leg.

WHERE DO YOU STORE A WEREWOLF?

In a were-house.

DO MUMMIES MAKE GOOD SKATEBOARDERS?

Yes, they really shred.

HOW DO VAMPIRES FALL ASLEEP?

They count Draculas.

WHY DID FRANKENSTEIN CARRY A PICKET SIGN?

He heard there was a demon-stration.

WHERE DOES GODZILLA BUY HIS CLOTHES?

At the maul.

KNOCK-KNOCK.

Who's there?

GHOST

Ghost who?

GHOST-AND IN THE CORNER!

WHAT HAPPENED WHEN THE BLOB APPEARED ON BROADWAY?
There were lots of ooze and aaahs.

WHY DID VULTURES KEEP COMING BACK TO THE LOUSY RESTAURANT?
The food was rotten.

WHAT DOES GODZILLA PUT ON LETTERS?
Stomps.

WHY WAS THE INVISIBLE MAN SAD?
His girlfriend said she couldn't see him anymore.

WHAT DO YOU SERVE A WITCH FOR DINNER?
A twelve-curse meal.

WHAT GHOSTS DO YOU FIND ON AIRPLANES?
Fright attendants.

DID THE WITCHES' TALENT SHOW SELL OUT?
Yes, it was standing broom only.

WHY DID THE CYCLOPS GIVE UP TEACHING?
He only had one pupil.

TOP TEN

WAYS TO TELL YOUR TEACHER IS A VAMPIRE

1. He has a bat attitude.

2. Always "hanging" with his friends.

3. Organizes a blood drive.

4. Opens a can of pineapple juice with his teeth.

5. Discourages you from wearing turtlenecks.

6. Shops at Bed, Bat & Beyond.

7. Always coffin.

8. Goes to "All You Can Eat Night" at the morgue.

9. Tells neck-neck jokes.

10. Has been a teacher since 1793.

CLOTHES CALL

Ha, ha. I'm putting you on!

DID YOU HEAR ABOUT THE SHIRT AND COLLAR THAT RAN A RACE?

It ended in a tie.

WHY DID THE GIRL GIVE HER COMPUTER A SWEATER?

In case it froze.

WHAT DID ONE PANTS LEG SAY TO ANOTHER?

"Let's split!"

WHY DID THE BREAD ROLL ENTER THE FASHION SHOW?

It wanted to be a roll model.

TEACHER: *You've got your shoes on the wrong feet.*
FRED: *But these are the only feet I've got!*

WHAT DID THE PRINCIPAL WEAR UNDER HER DRESS?
A permission slip.

WHAT DID THE SCARF SAY TO THE BLOUSE?
"You're under a vest."

WHAT'S THE SADDEST CLOTHING?
Blue jeans.

WHY DID THE PANTYHOSE HAVE HOLES?
They run in the family.

TEACHER: *Your socks are mismatched.*
JUDY: *I know. I have another pair like them at home.*

WHY DID THE PAINTER GO TO THE CLOTHING STORE?
He wanted a second coat.

WHAT DO LAWYERS WEAR UNDER THEIR PANTS?
Briefs.

TOP TEN

SIGNS YOU'RE SPENDING TOO MUCH TIME ON THE COMPUTER

1 When Mom serves broccoli, you try to bring up a different menu.

2 You're confused when the waiter says, "I'll be your server."

3 You try to play Angry Birds on your TV's remote control.

4 Instead of saying good night to your mom, you sign off.

5 You ask Santa if you can sit on his laptop.

6 You raise your hand to go to the chat room.

7 You're taking Tylenol for a computer virus.

8 You try to delete your little brother.

9 You wish you got more spam.

10 This is being read to you.

COUNTRY CLUB

Oh, gee . . . ography!

WHAT COUNTRY IS GOOD FOR FISH?

Finland.

SOME COUNTRIES ARE GOOD FOR UNCLES, SOME ARE GOOD ____.

France.

WHAT COUNTRY IS OUT OF BREATH?

Iran.

WHAT COUNTRY IS IN A HURRY?

Russia.

WHAT COUNTRY CAN'T STOP EATING?

Hungary.

WHAT COUNTRY WEARS A SUIT?

Thailand.

WHAT'S A PILGRIM'S FAVORITE COUNTRY?

Turkey.

WHAT COUNTRY IS SLIPPERY?

Greece.

WHAT COUNTRY THROWS ROCKS?

Estonia.

WHAT COUNTRY CRIES?

Wales.

WHAT COUNTRY HAS TWO KNEES?

Tunisia.

WHAT COUNTRY SUNBATHES?

Tanzania.

WHAT COUNTRY ISN'T FAKE?

Israel.

WHAT COUNTRY CAN'T CARRY A TUNE?

Singapore.

KNOCK-KNOCK.
Who's there?
KENYA.
Kenya who?
KENYA LET ME IN
ALREADY?

Knock-knock.
Who's there?
Congo.
Congo who?
Congo out today.
Maybe tomorrow!

Knock-knock.
Who's there?
Norway.
Norway who?
Norway am I telling you
all my knock-knocks!

Knock-knock.
Who's there?
Samoa.
Samoa who?
Samoa French fries,
please!

Knock-knock.
Who's there?
Egypt.
Egypt who?
Egypt me, he'll gyp
you, too!

KNOCK-KNOCK.
Who's there?
TOGO.
Togo who?
BURGER. TO GO WITH
THE FRIES!

WHAT COUNTRY
MAKES YOU SHIVER?

Chile.

FRED'S SASSY ANSWERS TO
SILLY QUESTIONS

TEACHER: ARE YOU SLEEPING IN CLASS?
FRED: I WOULD BE IF YOU WEREN'T TALKING SO LOUD!

TEACHER: WHY DID YOU MISS SCHOOL YESTERDAY?
FRED: I GUESS I'M JUST ABSENT-MINDED.

JUDY: HOW'D YOU FIND THE WEATHER?
FRED: I JUST WENT OUTSIDE AND IT WAS THERE.

TEACHER: WHY IS YOUR HEAD ON YOUR DESK?
FRED: YOU SAID TO KEEP MY EYES ON MY OWN PAPER!

TEACHER: ARE YOU SPITTING?
FRED: NO, PRACTICING TO BE A LAWN SPRINKLER.

TEACHER: WHY ARE YOU LATE AGAIN?
FRED: THEY'RE ALWAYS RINGING THE BELL BEFORE I GET THERE.

TEACHER: CAN I HAVE A WORD WITH YOU?
FRED: WHICH ONE?

TEACHER: DID YOU TAKE THE BUS HOME?
FRED: NO, IT WON'T FIT IN OUR GARAGE.

EXCUSE ME, DO YOU HAVE THE RHYME?

Hey, homies! What do you call . . .

TEXTED TEST ANSWERS?
A CHEAT TWEET.

AN INSTRUCTOR WITH TWO HEADS?
A CREATURE TEACHER.

A HIP MEASURING STICK?
A COOLER RULER.

AN EXAM-EATING BUG?
A TEST PEST.

A CRIME NOVEL THAT TAKES PLACE A HUNDRED YEARS AGO?
A HISTORY MYSTERY.

A GRADE REPORT BURNED IN A FIRE?
A CHARRED CARD.

A FAKE ATHLETE?
A MOCK JOCK.

AN EXAM THAT'S IRONED?
A PRESSED TEST.

A GRUESOME TALE?
A GORY STORY.

GOOD-BYE FROM FRED

Heyyy, here's one last joke for all my home dawgs:

What did the scary vampire music teacher say at the end of this book?

BAT'S ALL, FOLKS!

Yours Till the Ice Screams . . .

FRED